REPAIR SLIP
DAMAGED AT CHECKOUT

Crayon marks on inside cover
10/22
KH

CHANGE STATUS TO REPAIR AT CHECKIN

SEND TO SELECTOR

Status changed to repair

CIRCLE: ADS   OR   (KIDS)

SandCastle 2

Baby Animals

Puppies

Kelly Doudna

Publishing Company

Published by SandCastle™, an imprint of ABDO Publishing Company, 4940 Viking Drive, Edina, Minnesota 55435.

Printed in the United States.

Photo credits: Peter Arnold, Richard Hamilton Smith/Corbis, James L. Amos/Corbis, Lowell Georgia/Corbis, George Lepp/Corbis, Tony Arruza/Corbis, Wolfgang Kaehler/Corbis, MasterClips

Library of Congress Cataloging-in-Publication Data

Doudna, Kelly, 1963-
    Puppies / Kelly Doudna.
       p. cm. -- (Baby animals)
    Summary: Simple text and photographs present the physical characteristics and behavior of puppies.
      ISBN 1-57765-181-2
      1. Puppies--Juvenile literature. [1. Dogs. 2. Animals-
-Infancy.] I. Title. II. Series: Doudna, Kelly, 1963- Baby animals.
    SF426.5.D68 1999
    636.7'07--DC21   98-21704
                                                     CIP
                                                       AC

The SandCastle concept, content, and reading method have been reviewed and approved by a national advisory board including literacy specialists, librarians, elementary school teachers, early childhood education professionals, and parents.

Let Us Know

After reading the book, SandCastle would like you to tell us your stories about reading. What is your favorite page? Was there something hard that you needed help with? Share the ups and downs of learning to read. We want to hear from you! To get posted on the Abdo Publishing Company Web site, send us email at:

sandcastle@abdopub.com

About SandCastle™

Nonfiction books for the beginning reader

- Basic concepts of phonics are incorporated with integrated language methods of reading instruction. Most words are short, and phrases, letter sounds, and word sounds are repeated.

- Readability is determined by the number of words in each sentence, the number of characters in each word, and word lists based on curriculum frameworks.

- Full-color photography reinforces word meanings and concepts.

- "Words I Can Read" list at the end of each book teaches basic elements of grammar, helps the reader recognize the words in the text, and builds vocabulary.

- Reading levels are indicated by the number of flags on the castle.

Look for more SandCastle books in these three reading levels:

Level 1 (one flag)	Level 2 (two flags)	Level 3 (three flags)
Grades Pre-K to K	**Grades K to 1**	**Grades 1 to 2**
5 or fewer words per page	5 to 10 words per page	10 to 15 words per page

A young dog is
a puppy.

Puppies are small.

Sometimes puppies
look like each other.

Sometimes puppies
look different from
each other.

This puppy plays
with a stick.

This puppy runs and
plays outside.

This puppy plays with
two young friends.

This puppy and its mother are tired.

This puppy is ready
for a nap.

Do you have a pet?

Do you have a puppy?

Words I Can Read

Nouns

A noun is a person, place, or thing

dog (DAWG) p. 5
mother (MUH-thur) p. 17
nap (NAP) p. 19
pet (PET) p. 21
puppy (PUHP-ee)
pp. 5, 11, 13, 15, 17, 19, 21
stick (STIK) p. 11

Plural Nouns

A plural noun is more than one
person, place, or thing

friends (FRENDZ) p. 15
puppies (PUHP-eez) pp. 5, 7, 9

Verbs

A verb is an action or being word

are (AR) pp. 5, 17
do (DOO) p. 21
have (HAV) p. 21
is (IZ) pp. 5, 19
look (LUK) pp. 7, 9
plays (PLAYZ) pp. 11, 13, 15
runs (RUHNZ) p. 13

Adjectives

An adjective describes something

different (DIF-ur-ruhnt) p. 9
ready (RED-ee) p. 19
small (SMAWL) p. 5
tired (TYE-urd) p. 17
two (TOO) p. 15
young (YUHNG) pp. 5, 15

Sight Words

friends

stick

pet